ESSENTIALS OF GOOD SCIENTIFIC WRITING

GUIDE FOR STUDENTS, SCIENTISTS, ESL WRITERS, AND EDUCATORS.

JASMIN HOLM, Ph.D.

Introduction

We are not all born writers, but we can all learn the skills needed to produce good writing. The purpose of scientific writing is to describe, inform, and educate, and to do this effectively, you need to write clearly, concisely and ruthlessly.

By learning a few essential rules, paying attention to the writing of your peers, and practicing your own writing, you can master the skills needed to become a good and effective writer.

What makes a good writer

1. Read, pay attention, and imitate. Reading the work of your peers will educate you on the different ways you can express yourself. Pay attention on small gimmicks—such as the use of dash, parentheses, and semicolon—that allow you to emphasize structure and organize your sentences and paragraphs effectively.

2. Write, write, and write. You will only get better by practice. Write a journal, write mock papers, or be creative with your lab book.

3. Talk about your research before writing about it. Talking will force you to think how to clearly express yourself and your results. Ask yourself questions

about your research, and think how you can concisely answer those questions.

4. Write to engage your readers—not to bore them. Use active voice, alter paragraph structure, and use punctuation to emphasize certain words or phrases.

5. Stop waiting for inspiration—it might not come. Instead prepare for the writing by having a "prewriting" step.

6. Know that writing is hard for everyone (or at least most everyone).

7. REVISE!!!!!!!! Revision is probably the most important step that many authors forget to do.

8. Read your work out loud or read it backward (one sentence at a time).

9. Learn how to cut ruthlessly. Cut unnecessary words, rephrase, and eliminate long sentences.

10. Take risks. Don't stay within boundaries if you don't need to.

11. Always read the style instructions the particular journal or employer is expecting you to use. Using the wrong style manual can cause errors in your text even though they are grammatically correct.

12. Ask someone to read and edit your work. They don't need to be a professional editor to give pointers and suggestions.

What not to do – five major errors!

Scientific literature is often made more confusing than necessary. It is almost as authors think they need to use complicated sentences and fancy words to make their point.

But just because you are writing about a complex topic, such as science, your writing doesn't need to be complicated. In fact, most scientific journals prefer writing that is simple and easy to understand.

The main mistakes authors often make are:

1. Using confusing and long sentences
2. Writing in passive voice
3. Using unnecessary phrases and words
4. Turning your verbs as nouns
5. Not reading your writing out loud

When reading over your paper or a manuscript, you should be able to understand the point you are trying to make with little effort. If a sentence sounds complicated to you, it will be even more confusing to the reader.

You can improve your writing by simply reading your work out loud. Hearing your words, instead of reading them, will help you eliminate complicated sentence structures, grammatical errors, and unclear paragraphs and phrases.

ASK YOURSELF

- Is the sentence easy to understand?
- Does your message stand out?
- Are there any unnecessary words and phrases you can cut off?

This book goes over common mistakes authors make, and offers simple and easy-to-learn tips on how to improve your writing.

Principles of effective writing

USE THE ACTIVE VOICE

"Never use the passive where you can use the active"

- George Orwell –

Active voice is probably the clearest way to make a statement. It expresses a clause in which the subject does the action described by the verb. Active voice—as the name insinuates—makes your sentence lively and clear.

Reasons why you should use active voice when writing scientific, or any other type of text, include:

- Active voice is easier to read.
- It is a myth to avoid first-person pronouns - you did the experiments you can admit that
- As an author you are taking the responsibility of the content - using "we" or "our" will just clarify it
- Most journals ask to use active voice

The opposite of active voice, and a common error for many authors, is the use of passive voice. Passive voice draws attention to the subject or the object, rather than the action (verb).

Active voice:

> Subject-verb-object

"She drives the car"
"They made mistakes"
"She ran the company"

Passive voice:

> Object-verb-subject

"The car was driven by her"
"Mistakes were made"
"The company was run by her"

Characteristics of passive voice:

- Passive verb = a form of a verb "to be" + the past participle of the main verb
- The main verb must be a transitive verb = meaning, take an object

"To be" verbs	
is	could be
are	shall be
was	should be
were	will be
be	would be
Been	may be
Am	might be
	must be
	has been

Examples (object *verb* <u>subject</u>)

Passive: "My first visit to Finland will always be *remembered* by <u>me.</u>"

Active "<u>I</u> will always *remember* my first visit to Finland."

Examples (object *verb*) – missing <u>subject</u>

Passive: "Toy ads *were designed* to appeal children"

Active: "<u>We</u> designed the toy ads to appeal children"

How to fix.

1. Ask: "Who does what to whom"
2. Use "we" (or "I")
3. Be direct

When to use passive voice

Methods section - what was done is more important than who did it.

- Readers skim the section for key words
- Not worth of all the effort to use active voice.

Examples:

Passive:
The cancer drug was found harmful, and the patients were taken off the treatment straightaway. The study was interrupted and the patients were cared for their injuries.

Active:
We found the cancer drug harmful, and took the patients off the treatment straightaway. We interrupted the study and cared the patients for their injuries.

———————

Passive:
General dysfunction of the immune system has been suggested at the white blood cell level in human studies.

Active:
Human studies suggest a general immune dysfunction at the white blood cell level.

———————

Passive:
By applying a high resolution magnet downstream of the laser electron interaction region, the spectrum of the electron beams could be observed.

Active:
We could observe the spectrum of the electron beams by applying a high resolution magnet downstream of the laser electron interaction region.

CUT THE CLUTTER

"A medical paper should be like a lady's dress – short enough to be interesting but long enough to cover the subject"

- Anonymous -

Scientific papers often contain more words and sentences than actually needed to deliver the message. Clear and concise manuscripts often follow the rule "less is more."

When you learn how to eliminate non-informative and unnecessary words and phrases: your writing will be more effective in delivering your message, and your readers will be pleased.

Dead weight phrases

Authors often want to begin their sentence with an elaborative phrase that offers no real information. This causes distraction from the main point, making the sentence long and confusing.

You should avoid verbosity in all situations and opt for a more simple and precise way to make your point.

ASK YOURSELF

- Do you need the phrase to make your point?
- Is your message clear without the phrase?
- Can you replace the phrase with a simple word?

Examples of unnecessary phrases

- As it is well known
- It has been shown
- Studies have shown
- It should be emphasized
- The purpose of
- In the present report
- Based on the results
- Studies pertaining to

Example:
Based on the results we can conclude that option B would elicit *difficulties* in *obtaining* the necessary tools, and *challenges* in *finding* appropriate solutions to the problem.

Fix:
We conclude that option B would elicit challenges in finding necessary tools and appropriate solutions to the problem.

> **Example:**
> As it is well known, obesity increases the risk of many health conditions. This is why we need to educate people about healthy eating habits.
>
> **Fix:**
> Obesity increases the risk of many health conditions and this is why we need to educate people about healthy eating habits.

Empty words and adverbs

Adverbs are modifiers that are used to describe how, where, when, and how often. Authors often use these "empty weight" words to emphasize certain verbs or adjectives in their text. However, these words are often unnecessary and do not provide any additional information. In addition, they can often leave the reader asking "why" or "how much"?

ASK YOURSELF

- Do you need the word to emphasize your phrase or to make your point?

Examples of empty words:

- Important (how important?)
- Essential
- Generally
- Basically
- Actually
- Fortunately
- Very
- Really
- Quite
- Quickly
- Carefully
- Easily

Example:
Studies have shown that obesity rates are **generally** increasing and thus, it is **very important** we promote healthy eating habits.

Fix:
Studies show that obesity rates are increasing, thus we need to promote healthy eating habits.

Long phrases that could be short

Long phrases often cause distraction from the main point of your message. Replace wordy phrases with a shorter phrase or a word. This will make the sentence shorter, easier to read, and makes your point stand out clearly.

Table 1. How to replace wordy phrases.

Wordy phrase	Short form
Have an effect on	Affect
Give rise to	Cause
Due to the fact that	Because
The amount of 2 mg	2mg
The case of meningitis	Meningitis
The extent of damage	Damage
The magnitude of 3-fold	3-fold
The purpose of this study	This study
A majority of	Most
Are of the same opinion	Agree
Less frequently occurring	Rare
All four of the	The four

Example:
Due to the fact that the results showed protection a majority of time with treatment A and not with treatment B, we concluded treatment A to be the preferable choice.

Fix:
Because protection mostly occurred with treatment A, we concluded it to be the preferable choice.

Repetitive words or phrases

Sometimes authors tend to repeat their message within the same sentence or in two consecutive sentences. Although sometimes this might be needed to clarify your message, most of the time you can make your point with a better structured sentence, without the need to repeat yourself.

ASK YOURSELF

- Do you need to repeat the information?
- Is the first sentence clear enough to make your message or can you modify it?
- Can you reconstruct a sentence so you don't need to repeat a similar word within the sentence?

Examples of repetitive words

- illustrate and demonstrate
- challenge and difficulty
- studies and examples
- increase and enhance
- decrease and reduce
- obtain and find
- showed and found
- teaches and guides

Example; Repetitive sentences:

We found that x antibody showed protection in a dose-dependent manner, unlike the y antibody, which showed no protection. Our results showed that x antibody was protective, while the y antibody was non-protective.

Fix:

Our results showed protection in a dose-dependent manner only with the x antibody, while the y antibody failed to protect.

Example; repetitive words in a sentence:

Based on the results we can conclude that option B would elicit difficulties in obtaining the necessary tools, and challenges in finding appropriate solutions to the problem.

Fix:

We conclude that option B would elicit challenges in finding necessary tools and appropriate solutions to the problem.

Eliminate negatives

A negative sentence states something is incorrect and uses the term "not" to cancel the validity of the sentence. However, negative sentences are wordy and can often be complicated and confusing. Avoid the use of negative sentences to improve the clarity of your sentences.

Any sentence that uses "not" can usually be turned around to a positive statement.

Table 2. Example of how to eliminate negatives.

Negative	Positive
Not honest	Dishonest
Not harmful	Safe
Not important	Unimportant
Did not succeed	Failed
Did not remember	Forgot
Did not pay attention	Ignored
Does not have	Lacks

Examples:

Negative: He was not usually right
Positive: He was usually wrong

Negative: They did not believe the treatment was harmful.
Positive: They believed the treatment was safe.

Eliminate "there is" and "there are"

Starting sentences with the phrase "there is" and "there are" is a common practice among scientists. However, when you do this you are using a sentence structure called an expletive construction, and not the typical subject-verb-object construction.

This can be confusing since "there" is not a subject but just a filler word.

Examples:
There are many ways we can do the experiment.

Fix:
We can do the experiment in many ways.

_____

Example:
There were many colonies of bacteria in the plate.

Fix:
Many bacterial colonies grew on the plate.

_____

Example:
The data confirmed that there is an association between protein A and protein B.

Fix:
The data confirmed an association between protein A and B.

Examples

Example 1:

"This paper provides a review of molecular genetic study design, using as examples studies that illustrate the methodological challenges or that demonstrate the successful solutions to the difficulties in genetic research."

Problems with this paragraph:

1. **Verb is a noun**: "…provides a review…"— review is a noun
2. **Repetitive words:** "examples" and "studies" mean the same thing.
3. **Unnecessary words:** "methodological" does not give any new information.
4. **Repetitive words**: "illustrate" and "demonstrate" are synonyms.
5. **Unnecessary words:** "successful" is unnecessary—you cannot have an unsuccessful solution.
6. **Repetitive words**: "challenges" and "difficulties"

Cut the clutter

"This paper reviews molecular genetic study design, using examples that illustrate the challenges and solutions of genetic research."

Example 2:

Ultimately X4 guards **not only** against malignant tumors **but also** plays a role in developmental processes **as diverse as** differentiation, aging, and fertility.

Fix:

X4 protects against malignant tumors and plays a role in developmental processes, such as differentiation, aging, and fertility.

Or

Besides preventing cancer, X4 plays roles in differentiation, aging, and fertility.

Example3:

Injuries to the brain **have long been known to be** among the most devastating and expensive **of all injuries** to treat **medically**

Fix:

Brain injuries are among the most devastating and expensive to treat.

DO NOT TURN VERBS INTO NOUNS

Authors often use abstract nouns derived from verbs in their writing. This will take some of the strength of the verb and the sentence away.

- Don't kill verbs by making them into nouns

- Say exactly who does what to whom

Table 3. Examples of noun vs. verb forms.

Noun	Verb
Obtain estimates of	Estimate
Take an assessment of	Assess
Provide a review of	Review
Offer conformation of	Confirm
Showed cooperation	Cooperate
Provide interaction	Interact
Provides a description of	Describe
Was used for selection	Select
Provides activation of	Activate
Was used for expression	Express
To have an effect	To affect
Investigation was carried out	Investigate
Evaluation was done	Evaluate

Nouns:

The **Identification** of the different types of lymphomas is important in the **discovery** of new therapies and **reduction** of mortality.

Verbs:

Identifying the different lymphomas will help **discover** new therapies and **reduce** mortality.

———————————

Nouns:

An **investigation** of the protective activities were carried out.

Verbs:

We **investigated** the protective activities.

Or

The protective activities **were investigated**.

———————————

Nouns:

Classification of the underlying causes was done to do an **estimation** of the impact of environmental factors to development of cancer.

Verbs:

We **classified** the underlying causes and **estimated** the impact of environmental factors to development of cancer.

DO NOT BURY THE MAIN VERB

- Readers are waiting for the main verb!

- Bring the main verb close to the subject - Having too much "stuff" between the subject and the main verb loses the readers.

Example:
A study of 100 adolescents with diabetes receiving treatment in one of two managed care settings **found** that only 67 percent had seeked for professional care for their symptoms.

Fix:
A study **found** that, of 100 adolescents with diabetes who received treatment in one of two managed care settings, only 67 percent had seeked for professional care for their symptoms.

Example:
The preliminary results, which were obtained using microscopic and flow cytometric techniques or experiments done in an in vivo animal model, **showed** protection.

Fix:
The preliminary results **showed** protection using microscopic and flow cytometric techniques or in vivo animal model experiments.

WRITE WITH STRONG VERBS

Use strong verbs

- Strong verbs make sentences lively and go.
- Use thesaurus to find the best verb.

Compare: **Weak verbs**
We **assessed** the effect of cancer drug B43 for its ability to **erase** pain, **lessen** nausea, and **advance** overall wellbeing.

With: **Strong verbs**
We **evaluated** the effect of cancer drug B43 for its ability to **eliminate** pain, **reduce** nausea, and **improve** overall wellbeing.

Compare: **Weak verbs**
The cancer drug **was found** harmful, and the patients **were taken off** the treatment straightaway. The study **was interrupted** and the patients **were cared for** their injuries.

With: **Strong verbs**
We **deemed** the cancer drug harmful, and **took** the patients off the treatment immediately. We **discontinued** the study and **treated** the patients for their injuries.

Use "to be" verbs purposefully and sparingly

IS, ARE, WAS, WERE, BE, BEEN, AM...

Compare:

General dysfunction of the immune system has been suggested at the white blood cell level in human studies.

With:

Human studies suggest a general immune dysfunction at the white blood cell level.

AVOID ACRONYMS AND ABBREVIATIONS

Many researches use acronyms and or abbreviations for the scientific terms involved in their research. However, although you are familiar with the abbreviation, your audience may not be. Thus, using acronyms and abbreviations can be confusing and make a good article hard to read.

In general, you should avoid using acronyms and abbreviations unless:

- They are universally known and used (such as HIV, DNA, IgG, mAb, and FDA)
- You are using the term more than five times in the paper.
- They improve the clarity and readability o the text.

Before using acronyms or abbreviations, ask yourself whether they are truly needed to improve the clarity of the manuscript. If the answer is "no"—then do not use them. In addition, only use them for one or two of the MOST COMMON terms and not for any other terms (even if mentioned more than five times).

Always introduce the acronym or abbreviation when first used (followed by placing the acronym or abbreviation in parentheses).

> Examples:
>
> Immunoglobulin G (IgG) is the most common Ig type in blood.
>
> According to the Federal Drug Administration (FDA), antihistamines should not be used for this condition.

Do not introduce the same acronym or abbreviation twice in the same manuscript, EXCEPT in:

- Abstract
- Tables and figures
- Any other section in the paper that needs to stand alone.

Note! The use of common abbreviations can vary depending whether the word is a noun or an adjective. For example, United States should only be abbreviated as U.S. when used as an adjective, and spelled out when used as a noun.

Table 4. Abbreviations as noun or adjective.

adjective	noun
U.S. dollar	in the United States
US economy	United States is

Important Grammar Tips

Common grammatical errors made in science writing

Singular vs. plural words

Table 5. Nouns that originated from Greek and Latin are often used in the wrong form.

Singular	Plural
Alga	Algae
Bacterium	Bacteria
Fungus	Fungi
Datum	Data
Medium	Media
Nucleus	Nuclei
Analysis	Analyses
Focus	Foci
Formula	Formulae
Genus	Genera
Hypothesis	Hypotheses
Larva	Larvae
Parenthesis	Parentheses
Stimulus	Stimuli
Synthesis	Syntheses

Examples:

You cannot say "**data is**" or "**data shows**"

Say:
The data are
Our data show
The data support

———————

You cannot say "the **media was** made"

Say:
The **medium was** made
The **media were** used

———————

You cannot say "**Analysis were** performed"

Say:
Analysis was performed
Analyses were performed

———————

You cannot say "**Bacteria is** a unicellular"

Say:
Bacterium is a unicellular micro-organism.
Bacteria are sensitive to antibiotics.

Alternate vs. alternative

Alternate, which can be a noun or a verb, refers to things occurring in series.

Alternative is a noun and means "different choice."

Affect vs. effect

> **Affect** is verb (affect as a noun means feeling)
> **Effect** is noun

> Example: **verb**
> Wrong: The class effected her
> Correct: The class affected her
>
> Example: **noun**
> Wrong: The class had an affect on her
> Correct: The class had an effect on her

Compared to vs. compared with

> **Compared to**: points out **similarities** between **different** things (not generally used in science writing)

> "The buildings are not tall compared to him"
> "I will compare you to a summer's day"

Compared with: points out **differences** between **similar** things

> "IgG3 had higher affinity when compared with IgG2b"
>
> "Brain tumors are relatively rare compared with more common cancers"

Concentration vs. level

Concentration refers to a measured amount of something (such as drug, chemical, and substance) in a unit of another substance (such as blood or water)

Level refers to position or rank on a scale or a relative degree of intensity or achievement.

For example

> **Wrong:** Cholesterol level was 30 mg/dL.
>
> **Correct:** Cholesterol concentration was 30 mg/dL.
>
> **But**
>
> Your cholesterol levels are high (refers to a ranking).

That vs. which

That is the **restrictive** (defining) pronoun

Which is the **nonrestrictive** (non-defining) pronoun

> **The _vial_ *that* contained the mouse DNA was broken.**

→There are many vials and you are telling specifically which one was broken.

> **The _vial_, *which* contained the mouse DNA, was broken.**

→Only one vial exists. You can remove the "which contained the mouse DNA" without changing the meaning of the sentence.

ASK YOURSELF

- Is the clause essential or non-essential!

- *That* - identifies "which one of many"

- *Which* - tells additional info about a specific thing

Since vs. because

Since implies that time has passed.

Because implies cause and effect.

> **Examples:**
>
> Many things changed since you left.
>
> Many things changed because you weren't here to stop them.

While vs. whereas

While implies an action that occurred at the same time as something else.

Whereas is used for comparisons.

> **Examples:**
>
> Mike stayed in the car, while Brandy went into the store
>
> Drug A was blue, whereas drug B was white.
>
> **Not**
>
> Drug A was blue, while drug B was white.

Less vs. fewer

Less and fewer are adjectives that are used to compare quantity or number.

Less is used to compare a quantity or size that cannot be counted individually.

Fewer is used to compare numbers or units that can be counted.

Examples:

The patient drank **less** water after the test.

The patient drank **fewer** glasses of water after the test.

Disk vs. disc

Disk refers to the material between vertebrae.

Disc refers to CD or DVD disc.

Different from vs. different than

It is always *different from*. Something cannot be different than something else.

Whether vs. if

Use *whether* in the context of distinct choices.

Use *if* for conditional context

Examples:

We examined whether drug A was more effective than drug B

Cancel the experiment if you feel shortness of breath.

Mucus vs. mucous

Mucus is a noun, mucous is an adjective

Collect mucus after administration of the drug.

Collect sample from the mucous membrane.

1990s vs. 1990's

1990s is plural, whereas 1990's is possessive.

The 1990s were filled with punk-style music.

The 1990's music was strange.

Of vs. for

Use *of* with a verb or a gerund.

Use *for* with a noun.

Examples:

Risk of getting infection increased.

Risk for infection remained the same.

Further vs. farther

Further is an extension of time or degree.

Farther refers to spatial distance.

Examples:

He threw the disc farther than her.

We further investigated the phenomenon

Homonyms

Homonyms are words that sound alike but have a different meaning.

Example: *its* vs. *it's*

Its is the possessive for of "it"

> The treatment was developed years ago, but its potential was only recently realized.

It's means "it is"

> The treatment was developed years ago, and it's now being used regularly.

Examples of other homonyms:

Breach	Breech
Discreet	Discrete
Lead	Led
Lessen	Lesson
Mucous	Mucus
Patience	Patient
Principal	Principle

Singular antecedents

Do not use "they" or "their" with a singular noun

Example:

"Each scientist worries about their results."

FIX 1: Use "her" or "his"

"Each scientist worries about her results."

FIX 2: Turn to plural

"Scientists worry about their results."

Ambiguous antecedents

Make sure you are making it clear to whom or what "it" or "them" refer to.

Example:
The second experiment was designed to contain 100 more mice than the first experiment. It tested two doses of the drug.

Fix:
The second experiment tested two doses of the drug and was designed to contain 100 more mice than the first experiment.

Punctuation

Dash, colon, semicolon, parenthesis

- Use them to vary your sentence structure

- Get creative with your sentence structure

- Punctuation has the power to separate two clauses – think of it as a length of a pause

Increasing power to separate:

Comma
Colon
Dash
Parentheses
Semicolon
Period

Semicolon

The semicolon gives a longer pause and a stronger emphasis on the second clause than the comma.

Semicolon is typically used:

- To connect two independent clauses or to join two ideas (typically not clauses joined by **and**).

> We verified her hypothesis; we failed to verify ours.
>
> She was treated at home; shortly, however, she had to be transferred to the hospital.
>
> In men the factor is diet; in women hormone deficiency.

- To separate items in lists that contain internal punctuation

> Studies were done in three groups: bacteria, mold, and fungi; mice, rats, and rabbits; and men, women, and children.

Parentheses

- Used to insert afterthought or explanation (a word, phrase, or sentence) into a passage that is grammatically correct without it.

- Used to add extra information that can be ignored by the reader without affecting the main point.

- Can be used to insert a definition, reference, dose, joke, and other "less significant" information

- When using parentheses remember:

> → If you remove the phrase within the parentheses, the main point of the sentence shouldn't change
> → Parentheses signal the reader they are allowed to skip over the phrase.

> Examples:
>
> High blood pressure (also called hypertension) can result from environmental factors (such as unhealthy diet and lack of exercise), as well as genetics.
>
> Mouse IgG is divided into four subclasses (IgG3, IgG1, IgG2b and IgG2a), while the IgM only has one subclass.

Colon

"The colon has more effect than the comma, less power to separate than the semicolon, and more formality than the dash"

- William Strunk Jr. -

- Used after an **independent clause** (clause has subject and a verb) to introduce a

    1. list
    2. quote
    3. explanation
    4. conclusion
    5. amplification

- Used to join two independent clauses if the second **amplifies** or **extends** the first (can sometimes be a choice between a colon and semicolon). When the first clause sets up for the second clause.

Example; list.

This project has a whole range of professionals: a doctor, a nutritionist, a statistician, and a computer specialist.

We used a variety of methods: HPLC, FACS, and ELISA.

Example; amplification

The scientist suffers from a common disease: lack of social skills.

Example; quote

She was an inspiration to our nation and her words: "we are what we make of ourselves," will carry to the future.

Example; two independent clauses

Companies use TOOLS for the same reason home buyers use mortgage brokers: the broker's knowledge and experience is supposed to help the client get the right deal.

Dash (em-dash)

"A dash is a mark of separation stronger than a comma, less formal than a colon, and more relaxed than parentheses."

- William Strunk Jr. -

- Used to add **emphasis** to information that is important—so it is opposite to parentheses (which bury the information).

- Used to insert an abrupt **definition** or **description** almost anywhere in the sentence—without confusing the reader.

- Dash allows long sentences to work without making them run on sentences.

- Dash is a powerful tool—just don't overuse it or it loses its impact.

Example; definition

The occurrence of high blood pressure—also called hypertension—has increased considerably over the recent years.

Example; long description

The results—which were verified by two different scientists in two different laboratories – indicated that the drug does not work.

Example; emphasis

The medications did more than prevent new fat accumulation. They also triggered obese patients to shed significant amounts of fat—up to half their body weight.

The results suggested that the protective ability of the drug depends on several factors— especially on the daily dose.

Note! The dash is similar to a hyphen (-) and has different forms of which the en-dash and em-dash are the most common:

> the em-dash or long dash (—)
> the en-dash or short dash (–)
> the hyphen (-)

The em-dash (with or without a space on either side) is used to separate clauses and is the dash mentioned earlier in this chapter.

The en-dash is typically considered as a substitute for "and" or "to"

> For example:
>
> 20–30 mg
> pp. 40–56
> 3:00–5:00 p.m.
> Antibody–antigen

The hyphen is used to join words (such as prefixes, compounds, and suspended hyphens) and to separate syllables of a single word.

Table 6. Different uses of the hyphen.

prefixes	post-traumatic
	pre-existing
	non-responsive
	intra-abdominal
compounds	Full-text article
	6-week study
	once-daily dose
	10-mg dose
suspended hyphens	large-scale study
	pre- and post-dose
	20-, 30-, and 40-year-olds
Syllables	A-me-ri-can
	Bac-te-ri-um

PARALLELISM

Parallelism refers to the balance of a sentence that lists ideas joined by "and", "or", or "but."

Unparalleled sentence: list that does not match

> The enzymes were evaluated for several properties, including **association** with self, **interacting** with the substrate, and **cooperating** with the cofactor.

→ **The above list uses verbs in unparalleled forms**

Parallel Sentence:

> The enzymes were evaluated for several properties, including **association** with self, **interaction** with the substrate, and **cooperation** with the cofactor.
>
> or
>
> The enzymes were evaluated for several properties, including **associating** with self, **interacting** with the substrate, and **cooperating** with the cofactor.

How to fix:

- Make sure each item in the list is: subject - verb – object
- Make sure the tense and form of verbs, nouns and adjectives match.

Table 7. Examples of using verbs as nouns and their forms:

Singular	plural
Interaction	Interactions
Association	Associations
Activation	Activations

Table 8. Examples of forms and tenses of verbs

Plain	Third person	Past tense	Past particle	Present particle
Interact	interacts	interacted	interacted	interacting
Activate	activates	activated	activated	activating
bind	binds	Bound	bound	binding
protect	protects	protected	protected	Protecting

Nouns: We evaluated the enzyme for its interaction, protection, and activation.

Plain form: We evaluated the enzymes ability to interact, protect and activate.

Example:
If you want to be a good scientist, you must **study** hard, critically **think**, and you **should be** a good listener

Fix:
If you want to be a good scientist, you must **study** hard, **listen** well, and **think** critically.

→ all verbs have plain form (also imperative), verb clause

or

Fix:
If you want to be a good scientist, you must be a good **student,** a good **listener,** and a critical **thinker.**

→ verbs as nouns, adjective clause

Note: The "-ing" form of verbs (called the gerund) is also a noun form.

He was thinking (not "He thinking")
The mixing of the samples was performed first.

→ "mixing" used as a noun in a bad passive sentence.

→ Fix: "We mixed the samples first" or "The samples were mixed first")

PARAGRAPHS

"Vigorous writing is concise. A sentence should contain no unnecessary words, a paragraph no unnecessary sentences."

- William Strunk Jr. -

Paragraphs should be precise, short, and logical. Avoid jumping back and forth between ideas, and using unparalleled sentence structure.

1. One paragraph = one idea.

2. Keep them short.

3. Give away punch line early and not at the end when making your conclusion.

4. Use parallel sentence structure.

5. If necessary - use transition words.

   - but
   - if
   - soon
   - on the other hand
   - nevertheless
   - hence
   - furthermore
   - in addition
   - however.

6. Use logical flow of ideas

    1. Sequential time
    2. General → specific (take home message first, then into details)
    3. Logical arguments (if a then b → then write a then b)

7. Readers will remember the first and last sentence the best. Make the last sentence memorable: emphasize at the end.

ASK YOURSELF

- What is the main idea?
- Then make that clear in the first and last sentence.

Example:

> Abdominal pain is a symptom that almost everyone experiences. The International Pain Society (IPS) groups abdominal pain into two types based on its cause: acute abdominal pain and chronic abdominal pain. Acute abdominal pain is sudden and often caused by food poisoning. Chronic abdominal pain is a long term condition, often caused by gastric ulcers, gastritis, or stomach cancer.

Flow: general → specific and logical.

We first evaluated the ability of the antibodies to induce phagocytosis. Our results showed that the IgG induced higher phagocytosis than the IgM antibody. We next evaluated whether complement activation was needed to induce phagocytosis. Interestingly, our results showed that the presence of complement was not needed to induce phagocytosis by either IgG or IgM.

Flow: sequential time and logical.

THE WRITING PROCESS

When you have finished your experiments and have analyzed the data, it is time to start writing your manuscript, abstract or presentation. Split your writing process into four steps: prewriting, writing a draft, revising, and finishing a final version. This will keep you organized and makes the writing process more streamlined.

Prewriting

Prewriting is probably the most important step in your writing process. The purpose of the prewriting step is to get you ready for the actual writing step.

    a.   Collect and organize your information

       → Gather all your information, including references, data, and lab notebooks.

    b.   Brainstorm the take-home message—what do you want say with this manuscript!

       → Write down your hypothesis and goals, print it out, and place somewhere visible.

       → Read your hypothesis and goals anytime you think you are drifting away from your topic, you are unsure what you want to say, or you forget what your main point is. This gets you back on track, and ensures you are not drifting away from the main point.

c. Make an outline:
   1) Plan your figures and tables.
   2) Figure out the flow of your message and the order of your figures and tables (figure 1, figure 2…).

d. Make your figures and tables, and then start building your first draft around them.

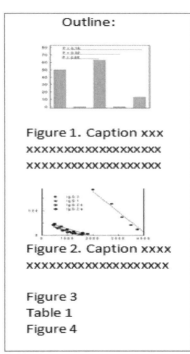

Outline:

Figure 1. Caption xxx
xxxxxxxxxxxxxxxxxxx
xxxxxxxxxxxxxxxxxxx

Figure 2. Caption xxxx
xxxxxxxxxxxxxxxxxxxx

Figure 3
Table 1
Figure 4

Writing the first draft

"Get through the first draft as quickly as possible."

- Joshua Wolf Shenk -

> **The main purpose of the first draft is to get your ideas on the paper – nothing more, nothing less!**

- Typical order for writing scientific manuscript is:
    1. Tables and figures
    2. Results
    3. Methods
    4. Introduction
    5. Discussion
    6. Abstract

- Writing a draft will make your life easier at the end.

- The purpose of a first draft is to get your ideas and thoughts on the paper in complete sentences.

- When it comes to the final version—less is more. This is not the case with the first draft. At this point on your writing process, you should write all your ideas down.

- Remember that you can always add, revise and remove information you have written down.

- When writing a first draft don't be a perfectionist!

  → This means you do not have to pay attention to your sentence structure, voice, or style as much— the purpose is to get your message on the paper.

"Be willing to write really badly."

- Jennifer Egan -

Revision

"Look for all fancy wordings, and get rid of them."

- Jacques Barzun -

Revision brings the elegance to your writing. It is needed to polish your writing to the point that you can submit your work.

Tips for revision:

1. Read your work out loud.

→ The brain processes the spoken word differently than written word.

→You can pick out most grammatical errors and confusing sentences by doing this.

2. Get rid of clutter.

→ Eliminate dead weight words and phrases, and adverbs.

→Eliminate long and confusing sentences.

→Replace wordy phrases.

→Eliminate repetitive words.

3. Check your verbs.

→Underline the main verb in each sentence.

→Watch out for passive verbs and buried verbs.

→Use the thesaurus to pick strong verbs.

4. Do organizational review.

→ Go through each paragraph and write the main points onto the margin. Then move paragraphs around to establish a logical flow.

5. Get feedback from others.

→ It is typically hard to edit your own work.

→ An outsider should be able to get the take-home message, main findings, and the significance of your work.

6. Take a break for a day or two and read again.

→ You will easily be blinded by the errors of your work if you keep reading the same paragraphs over and over again. Taking a break will allow your brain to "forget" and then take a "fresh look" to your writing.

Final draft

Do a final check for:

1. **Consistency**
   - Ensure your results and data are accurate.
   - Ensure you are using the same terms throughout the paper (e.g. you are not using two forms to describe the same thing, such as mAb and MAb)

2. **Numerical consistency**
   - Ensure that the numbers in your manuscript match.

     → e.g. numbers stated in your abstract match the numbers in your results and figures.
   - Ensure you are not using the word "significant" without a statistical comparison.

     → use "considerable" instead (e.g. considerable differences).

3. **Accuracy of your references**
   - Ensure you have cited the correct source.

     →e.g. paper x instead of paper y.
   - Ensure you have not misinterpreted the findings of the reference.
   - Ensure you are citing principle source not a secondary source.

     →Always assume other writers have made a mistake when citing a source!

     →Always go to the primary source!

CONSTRUCTING A GOOD MANUSCRIPT

Tables and figures

- Tables and figures are the most important part of your manuscript!
  → They are the foundation of your manuscript.

- Tables and figures need to stand alone and tell a complete story.
  →The reader shouldn't need to refer back to the main text when going over the figures and tables, and reading the captions and titles.

- Use figures to show trends and patterns; use tables to give precise values.

Figures

- Primary figures: gels, photographs, pathology slides, etc.
- Graphs: line graphs, bar graphs, scatter plots, histograms, survival curves, etc.

- Drawings and diagrams: used for illustrating work-flow, explaining experimental set up, giving hypothetical model, etc.

Tables

- Contains title, footnotes and the data.
  → follow the style guidelines of the particular journal you are submitting

Example table – common format.

Table 1. Summary of the study groups, and mean blood pressures measured during the study.

Characteristics	Treatment group	Control group
N	30	32*
Mean age (SE)	55.0 (10.0)	53.0 (12.0)
Female (%)	15.0 (50.0)	16.0 (50.0)
Mean BMI (SE)	22.0 (4.0)	24.0 (6.0)
Mean systolic BP (SE)		
Day 0	160 (12)	162 (12)
Day 14	155 (10)	160 (10)
Day 30	130 (8)	158 (13)

N= total number of patients enrolled, SE = standard error, BMI= body mass index, BP= blood pressure
*Out of 33 patients enrolled, 32 finished the trial

Tips

- Usually three lines: one under title, one before data and one under the table (above the footnotes). No grid lines.
- Give numbers using appropriate decimals (generally one to two).
- Explain abbreviations in the footnotes.

Example table – what not to do!

Table 1. Summary of the study groups, and mean blood pressures measured during the study.

Characteristics	Treatment group	Control group
N	30	32*
Mean age (SE)	55.077 (10.987)	53 (12)
Female (%)	15 (50)	16 (50)
Mean BMI (SE)	22.098 (4.098)	24 (6)
Mean blood pressure		
Day 0	160 (12)	162 (12)
Day 14	155 (10)	160 (10)
Day 30	130 (8)	158 (13)

*Out of 33 patients enrolled, 32 finished the trial

Fix:

- Remove grid lines.
- Make numbers match! Some numbers given without decimals some with three decimals (also three decimals not necessary for this data).
- Abbreviations need to be explained—the table needs to stand alone!

Results

The result section should:
- Summarize the data.
- Point out simple relationships.
- Highlight key numbers, not repeat numbers already shown in tables and figures.
- Describe trends.
- Avoid repeating the data presented in tables and figures, instead reference to the tables and figures.
- Be written in active voice.
- Be written in past tense: "we found", "results showed."

  → Only use present dense for items that continue to be true - Figure 3 shows, we believe, the data suggest, the findings confirm.

Tips:
- Break results into subsections with headings (unless the journal guidelines instruct otherwise).
- Complement information presented in tables and figures, e.g. mention data that is not shown.
- Generally do not write what you did – this is for the methods section.
- Use the term "significant" when talking about statistically significant data.
- Talk about control results, especially if not shown in figures and tables.

- Do not talk about the meaning of your results – this is for the discussion.

Example:

"Total of 30 patients was enrolled in the treatment group, and 32 in the control group. The average age of the patients was 55 ± 10, and 53 ± 12, respectively. Both groups consisted 50 percent of male and 50 percent of female. The mean systolic blood pressure at the beginning of the study was 160 ± 12 in the treatment group and 162 ± 12 in the control group, and at the end of the study (Day 30) 130 ± 8 and 158 ± 13, respectively. The difference in the systolic blood pressure between the treatment group and control group was statistically different ($p < 0.001$) at the end of the study. These results suggest the treatment lowers blood pressure significantly within 30 days."

Fix:

"The systolic blood pressure of the treatment group decreased from 160 to 130 ($P < 0.001$) during the 30 day treatment period (Table 1). We measured no significant change in the systolic pressure during the trial period in the control group (Table 1). The systolic blood pressure at the end of the study was statistically different ($p < 0.001$) between the treatment group and the control group."

Materials and Methods

Materials and methods should:

- Give a clear overview of how the experiments were done.

- Give enough information so that the experiments can be replicated.

- Written in passive voice
  → Passive voice gives emphasis to the method not who did the work.

- Written in past tense
  →Exception "data are summarized as"

- Should go over **who, what, when, where, how** and **why** questions that apply.

- Indicate how statistical analyses were done.

- Make it simple:
  - Break into smaller sections
  - Cite common methods, instead of repeating everything from step to step
  - Use a table or a flow chart

Introduction

- Should be between two to five paragraphs long.

- Summarize without going into specific details – leave that for discussion.

- It should not be an extensive review of your topic but rather focus on the specific hypothesis / aim of your study.

- Write clearly for general audience.

- General order:
    1. Background: what is known so far (roughly 1-2 paragraphs).
    2. Limitations and gaps in the knowledge: what is unknown (roughly 1-2 paragraphs).
    3. Hypothesis: aim of the study (0.5 paragraphs).
    4. Approach: proposed solution (0.5 paragraphs).

- Should be written in past tense: "they found," "et al. showed."

- Do not answer the research question and do not give results.

Discussion

- Should be written in active voice.

- Should focus on what your data proved and not drift too far away from the point.

- Should be clear and consistent: write in logical order.

- General order:
  1. Answer your hypothesis: "we found that."

  2. Back up your hypothesis with your data, and previous data. Compare your results to previous results.

  3. Defend your conclusion: what do your results mean and why are they important. Mention limitations and suggest future directions.

  4. Give the take-home message and importance of the study.

  5. End with a strong conclusion—restate your main finding

- Should be written in past tense: "we found." Except when talking about the implications of the data: "our data suggest."

Abstract

Abstract is the overview of the study. It should:

- Highlight something from each section of the paper.
- Be between 100 to 300 words long.
- Stand on its own—it is often the only thing people read.
- Contain keywords
- General order:

  1. Background (importance of study question)
  2. Hypothesis / objective
  3. Study design/ summary of main experiments
  4. Summary of key results
  5. Conclusion and take-home message
  6. Implications and speculations

- Each section around 1 to 2 sentences.

- May contain subheadings depending on the journal guidelines

Creating a Good Title

Title is the "face" of your manuscript and the first thing to capture the attention of your reader. After performing a keyword search, readers quickly glance through the list of papers by reading the title.

If your title doesn't grasp attention, is confusing, or fails to describe your research effectively, it is not likely to encourage the reader to go to the next step – which is to read the abstract.

This is why you need a title that is **clear, concise and effectively summarizes your research.**

A good title should:

- Be short and concise—do not try to include every detail of your research into the title.

- Be free of clutter and unnecessary words, such as "a study of," "an investigation of," or "development of."

- Be informative of your research.

- Use keywords.

- Avoid abbreviations that are not universally known.

Example:

The development of novel polymerase chain reaction for detecting and evaluating active MNG infection in mice.

Fix:

Novel polymerase chain reaction for detecting active meningitis.

Example:

Evaluation of the effects of calcium supplementation in diabetic patients for preventing obesity.

Fix:

Effects of calcium supplementation for obesity prevention in patients with diabetes: A randomized controlled trial.

Note: Randomized controlled trials (RCTs) should follow the Consolidated Standards of Reporting Trials (CONSORT) guideline, which aims to increase transparency in trial reporting, and helps authors to report trials in a standardized manner. The CONSORT checklist can be accessed at http://www.consort-statement.org/.

Quick Reference to English Grammar

Pronouns

Type	Singular	Plural
Subjective pronouns	I, you, he, she, it	we, you, they
Objective pronouns	Me, you, him, her, it	Us, you, them
Relative pronouns	Who, whom, whoever, whomever, whose, that, which	That, which, whichever, whosever
Interrogative pronouns	Who, whom, whose, which, what	
Reflexive pronouns	Myself, yourself, himself, herself, itself	Ourselves, yourselves, themselves

Rules:

Who should be used when referring to people.

That and *which* should be used when referring to objects or animals.

That is used to connect restrictive clause to the main clause.

Which is used to connect non-restrictive (non-essential) clause to the main clause.

Except, *which* can be used to connect restrictive clause when it is the object of a preposition: **of which, in which, to which, through which**.

Examples:

Matt, who did the experiment, found an old pair of sneakers in the lab.

The vial that contained the bacteria is missing?

The vial, which contains the virus, is missing?

The vial in which the bacteria were stored went missing.

Whose is the only possessive relative pronoun that can be used for both people and things.

Whom is used when a preposition precedes the word, or when it is the object of a verb: **for whom, to whom, of whom**

Examples:

The patients, whose eyes turned red, were diagnosed with red eye disease.

The mice, whose fur was black, were sold.

Matt, whom I barely knew, is missing

Matt, who forgot the vial, is missing.

Possessive pronouns	#My, your, his, hers, our, their, whose, its	Mine, yours, his, hers, ours, theirs, whose

*use only when used alone

#use when possessive pronoun is modifying a noun or when it precedes a gerund (a verb ending in "ing", acting as a noun).

Examples:

The vial was yours.

Your vial is missing.

We heard your screaming.

Coordinating Conjunctions: FANBOYS

For
And
Nor
But
Or
Yet
So

Subordinating Conjunctions

after	in as much	than
although	in order that	that
as	just as	though
as if	lest	til
as long as	now	unless
as much as	now since	until
as soon as	now that	when
as though	now when	whenever
because	once	where
before	provided	whereas
even	provided that	where if
even if	rather than	wherever
even though	since	whether
if	so that	which
if only	supposing	while
if when		who
if then		whoever
		why

Adverbs

Adverbs describe (modify) verbs, adjectives and other adverbs.

They tell us how, when, where, to what extent, and why. Many are same as subordinating conjunctions.

Example of adverbs

How	competitively, quickly, urgently, well
When	after, before, daily, weekly, never, today
Where	Away, here, in, outside, somewhere, there
To what extent	Extremely, not, quite, rather, too, very,
Why	Why

More at:

http://www.enchantedlearning.com/wordlist/adverbs.shtml

Independent and Dependent Clauses:

	Independent	Dependent
Particles	Subject and verb (and object)	Subject and verb (and object)
Rules	Can stand alone as a sentence	Cannot stand alone as a sentence; add additional information to the main clause
	Two ICs can be united with a comma and coordinating conjunction, or with a semicolon and conjunctive adverb	DC is connected to IC with a subordinating conjunction
		Two DC can be connected with a relative pronoun
example	I survived	because I can swim.

Examples:

I survived because I can swim.
Because I can swim, I survived.

REFERENCES:

Strunk, William. *Elements of Style.* Ithaca, N.Y.: Priv. print. [Geneva, N.Y.: Press of W.P. Humphrey], 1918; Bartleby.com, 1999. www.bartleby.com/141/. Accessed 10/25/2012

Scientific Style and Format. The CBE Manual for Authors, Editors, and Publishers. Sixth Edition.

Merriam-Webster's Collegiate Dictionary. 11th ed. Springfield, MA: Merriam-Webster, Inc.; 2007.

Annesly. Thomas M. The Title Says It All. *Clinical Chemistry.* 2010 March; 56(3):357-360

Annesly. Thomas M. The Abstract and the Elevator Talk: A Tale of Two Summaries. *Clinical Chemistry.* 2010 April; 56(4):521 - 524

Annesly. Thomas M. "It was a cold and rainy night": Set the Scene with a Good Introduction. *Clinical Chemistry.* 2010 May; 56(5):708 – 713

Annesly. Thomas M. Who, What, When, Where, How, and Why: The Ingredients in the Recipe for a Successful Methods Section. *Clinical Chemistry.* 2010 June; 56(6):897 – 901

Annesly. Thomas M. Show Your Cards: The Results Section and the Poker Game. *Clinical Chemistry.* 2010 July; 56(7):1066 – 1070

Annesly. Thomas M. The Discussion Section: Your Closing Argument. *Clinical Chemistry.* 2010 November; 56(11):1671 – 1674

Resources:

American Association for Clinical Chemistry. Clinical Chemistry Guide to Scientific Writing. http://www.aacc.org/publications/clin_chem/ccgsw/Pages/default.aspx#

Adverbs list, Accessed on 2/12/13 at http://www.enchantedlearning.com/wordlist/adverbs.shtml

CONSORT Transparent Reporting of Trials. http://www.consort-statement.org/

INDEX

Made in the USA
Monee, IL
11 March 2021

62464454R00048